THE
SUCCESS
BOOK

BY JOHN RANDOLPH PRICE

Check your bookstore for the books and audios above.
Items with asterisks can be ordered through Hay House at
800-654-4126 • FAX: 800-650-5115

Please visit the Hay House Website at:
www.hayhouse.com

THE
SUCCESS
BOOK

JOHN RANDOLPH PRICE

Hay House, Inc.
Carlsbad, CA

Copyright © 1998 by John Randolph Price

Published and distributed in the United States by: Hay House, Inc.,
P.O. Box 5100, Carlsbad, CA 92018-5100
(800) 654-5126 • (800) 650-5115 (fax)

Edited by: Jill Kramer   *Designed by:* Jenny Richards

Library of Congress Cataloging-in-Publication Data

Price, John Randolph.
    The Success Book / John Randolph Price.
        p.   cm.
    ISBN   1-56170-474-1 (Tradepaper)
    1. Success—Religious aspects—Christianity. 2. New Thought.
    I. Title.
    BJ1611.2.P75   1998
    299' .93—dc21   97-32367
                                          CIP

ISBN 1-56170-474-1

01 00 99 98   4 3 2 1
First Printing, February 1998

Printed in the United States of America

✦ CONTENTS

The Success Book is the second in a series of five diminutive volumes to be published by Hay House featuring a compilation of my writings. Each book covers a particular topic and will follow the size and format of my previously published work, *The Abundance Book*.

Since this book encompasses the concept of *success*, our first order of business should be to define the word. Webster says that success is "a favorable or satisfactory outcome." That's not meaningful enough for me. How about "Success is the natural order of the universe, wholly ordained by God as a force for good to replace the effects of this world with divine Reality—to transform failure to fulfillment, lack to abundance, illness to wholeness, and discord to harmony as the Power moves through us to accomplish and achieve in accordance with the Law of Being." I first wrote that in a *Quartus Report* back in the early '90s and later incorporated it into my book *The Angels Within Us*.

Success is good fortune, a basic universal principle. It is triumph, one of the attributes of our True Nature. It is fulfillment, that which our Essential Self *is* in mind and manifestation. Failure does not exist in this universe; it is only a false belief in consciousness that, once dissolved, puts us back into the natural order of things.

Yes, success is our natural state, and we must focus our minds on the dynamically complete and total success of our Divine Consciousness, eternally expressing as all that is good, true, and beautiful in life. We need to keep in mind that success and failure cannot exist simultaneously. When we choose one, the other cannot be. We choose success and leave the other in its wake.

You will notice that I look at the attainment of success through various methods, some of which will appear repetitious. My objective in those cases is to show a different approach to working with the same basic principle. Also, other instructions may seem somewhat contradictory in terms of active-passive processes, and that's because I'm addressing different frequencies in consciousness—to help you fulfill your dreams wherever you may be in your spiritual awakening.

Perhaps Thoreau summed it up best: "If one advances confidently in the direction of his dreams, and endeavors to live the life which he has imagined, he will meet with a success unexpected in common hours. He will put something behind, will pass an invisible boundary; new, universal, and more liberal laws will begin to establish themselves around and within him, or the old laws will be expanded and interpreted in his favor in a more liberal sense; and he will live with the license of a higher order of beings."

Come, let's find that *license of a higher order of beings*. Let's put failure, labor-in-vain, and non-fulfillment behind us and step out from behind the curtains and accept all the good the universe has for us in the name of true success. It is time.

DEVELOPING A CONSCIOUSNESS FOR SUCCESS

You must have the consciousness for that which is desired. Without the consciousness, it cannot come to you; with the consciousness, it *must* come. Let's look at a basic outline for deepening our awareness, understanding, and knowledge of true success.

1. What do you desire in life? You must focus your thoughts on what you really want.

2. You must make a definite decision to *accept* the fulfillment of your desires.

3. Your desires cannot be fulfilled in the outer world of experience and form unless you

have the consciousness or mental equivalent for them.

4. The first step in building the mental equivalent is to recognize that the Divine Idea corresponding to your desire already exists in your Superconsciousness. This is intellectual awareness.

5. An intellectual awareness alone does not have sufficient power to shape the outer picture. Your feeling nature must also be brought into play. When the two are combined, a powerful reaction takes place in the subjective phase of mind, setting up a vibration that corresponds to the spiritual equivalent of fulfillment in your Superconsciousness.

6. This fusion of mind and heart along the lines of a particular desire-fulfillment—if protected from thoughts to the contrary—will develop into a conviction. The conviction or mental equivalent becomes the pattern through which the Creative Energy of Mind flows or radiates. As this Energy, Light, Power, or Substance passes through the pattern, it takes on all the attributes of the pattern and goes forth into the outer world to

manifest corresponding circumstances, experiences, and form.

7. Do not outline the way your desire is to be fulfilled; do not be concerned with how your good is to come forth. You must trust the wisdom and ingenuity of the Power, which is God.

8. You develop your subjective convictions through a dedicated program of contemplative meditation, affirmations, and the proper use of your power of imagination.

9. Be filled with a sense of thankfulness and gratitude that your desires are *already* fulfilled (they are in Mind), and that they will come forth into visibility in the right time and in the right way.

10. Be active! If you just sit around and wait for your good to fall into your lap, your lap may be far removed from the point of contact and channel that the Power has selected specifically for the outpouring of your good.

Now let's put these ideas into a workable program that will enlarge and uplift your consciousness so that you may *release* all the good that is already yours.

Remember that desires come forth as an activity of your Higher Self, stirring you up to realize that it wants to do more for you—through you. When you want something that cannot hurt you or anyone else and will bring good into your life, it is your spiritual Self tugging at your heart's door trying to get your attention.

Now let's move from desire to decision. For every desire you have, you must make a firm, definite decision to accept the fulfillment of that desire. This is "claiming your good"—or choosing what is to be. Know that the Spirit within you loves a made-up mind, for this is where the pattern of fulfillment begins. In translating your desires into decisions, you must understand that everything already exists as a Pattern or Ideal in your Superconsciousness. To put it another way, *you already have the fulfillment of every desire, otherwise you could not have desired it in the first place.*

There is a divine idea corresponding to every form or experience in your life. Right now in the imaging Mind of your Inner Self is the idea of Abundant Prosperity. The Ideal Body is there, too, along with True Place success, Right Action, Companionship, Protection, Safety, Beauty,

Justice, and whatever else that would correspond to your desires—automobiles, homes, food, clothing. Remember that nothing in the world could exist unless it was first a spiritual idea. So in truth, you have everything right now. But in order for the Perfect Images to manifest in the material world, you must build a bridge. You must open a channel to release this "imprisoned splendor."

You start with recognition. The Superbeings identify and unify with the Power within and actually become it in expression. They examine every attribute of their Superminds, and they see unlimited prosperity, unlimited success, unlimited health, unlimited love, unlimited intelligence, unlimited power, unlimited everything—and they say: *What you are, I am.* They saturate their minds and hearts with this truth to such an extent that they constantly think and feel it.

You, too, can begin to build the bridge and open the channel with the very simple act of mentally recognizing that your True Self exists within you now, has everything for you, and will never leave you. Say to yourself:

There is a Presence and a Power within me now.
It is all-knowing, all-caring, all-loving,

all-powerful. It is the Completeness of the
Universe individualized as me. It is who I am.
It is what I am. It is God as me now.

Close your eyes for a moment, relax completely, and direct your attention to a point down behind
your physical heart and contemplate the idea—*I
am love.* Your physical heart really doesn't have
anything to do with it, but that region of your body
is the seat of your feeling nature; and the warmth,
the particular vibration you feel, is more of your
spiritual nature rising to the surface. You are actually becoming conscious of a Presence within
you...and the Presence is able to move into your
awareness with greater ease through the feeling of
Love, which is Its Nature.

You are now one with the Presence, and you
are beginning to feel the divine energy currents
flow in and through you. Recognize that within
this Feeling, which is the Presence, is the fulfillment of every desire. Know that right where you
are is the Mind of completeness. Let's use
"Success" as our Mind Model objective and see
how this Truth can be outpictured in our lives. Say
to yourself with a feeling of love and joy:

I have made a firm and definite decision in my mind to be wonderfully successful. I now accept the Truth that the spiritual Idea of True Place Success, the Divine Plan for me, is right where I am, in the Mind of my Inner Self.

This Self knows Itself to be a unique expression of God. It knows Its true worth. That Self is who and what I am. I unify with it. Therefore, I am Success. I am Prosperity.

I know that as I recognize and accept the Divine Plan for my life, which is already the Reality of me, it becomes active in my consciousness. I feel its power, its strength, its dynamic urge to mani-fest itself in my world as new opportunity, as the right job, as the ideal career.

There is now unity between the inner world of Spirit and the outer world of form. I have embod-ied the idea of my True Place in this world. I have claimed my good, and it is now interpreting itself as the perfect visible expression of contentment, satisfaction, and joy in the service of others. I am total success. And it is so!

Do you understand what you are doing with this kind of affirmative thought, idea, or concept? You are "treating" your subconscious mind—your feeling nature—with a lesson in Truth. And as your subjective nature begins to believe this Truth, it stops believing in boredom, unfulfillment, and failure. When it accepts the Truth about you and your True Place Success, it sets up a Success Vibration—a new subjective attitude, a conviction, a mental equivalent that corresponds to the absolute Truth of you.

As within, so without. You must also understand and recognize that there is a universal Law of Cause and Effect operating through you. It is called the Law of Attraction, the Law of Correspondence, and the Law of Consciousness. They are all the same. The Law is actually a Creative Force. It is God-substance, the Light of Spirit, a Power that is constantly and forever flowing through you, picking up the particular vibrations of your consciousness and expressing those vibrations in visible form, experience, and circumstance.

The Power is completely impersonal, and when it flows through your newly developed energy field of success, it has no choice but to manifest your True Place for this point of time in your life. It does not make any difference how badly you have failed in the past, or how many mistakes you have made. It only knows how to create according to your NOW consciousness. But if it flows through a mental atmosphere clouded with ideas of disappointment, resentment, and underachievement, it must, by its very nature, arrange corresponding situations in your life. "As within, so without. As a man thinketh in his heart, so is he." You are what you think.

Imagination clears the path. If there were no conflicting subjective thoughts after you completed your treatment, the idea would immediately begin to outpicture itself. But if you are like most of us, you have built up quite a reservoir of negative thought patterns. You have kept the door of your mind open to them and have fed them with your thoughts, words, and deeds. So these mischievous little thought children have grown strong and have banded together into a gang of mental delinquents. They represent your primary idea of your success in life—or the lack of it—and if you are not doing what you love and loving what you do, you know they are doing their job.

Since the Creative Energy flowing from your Higher Self moves through your thought patterns, you must let the divine idea be established as the Master Pattern. This means that you have to protect the "I am Success" idea, keeping it at the center of your being, so to speak, while evicting the noisy thieves from your consciousness.

To keep the success idea in position—lined up with the Light—you must call on your power of imagination. With the proper use of imagination, you "lock in" the idea much as a slide is secured in a projector. Imagination also extends the idea from the center to the circumference of your consciousness, pushing the negative patterns out of the way and providing a clear path for the Power to follow.

In your mind, see yourself truly enjoying your work. See yourself being totally fulfilled in providing a genuine service to others. See yourself joyously moving up the ladder of success professionally, financially, and emotionally. See this picture as a work of art, with you as the artist. Sketch in every detail. Add color to it. Make it a masterpiece! Now feel it in your heart. Love it! Sense the excitement of being the success you want to be right now. Let the waves of enthusiasm roll through you. Feel the utter delight and happiness as you look at your masterpiece. It's yours! And it's all here now. Don't think about your desires being fulfilled at some later date. They are already fulfilled right now. They are fulfilled because you can see them fulfilled. And the time-frame between the invisible and visible is only as short or long as the degree of faith and trust in the Power. "He shall give thee the desire of thine heart." "I have ways that will astound you."

After you have devoted a few minutes to your ideal picture, say to yourself:

I now release my masterpiece to my Higher Self, knowing that my Self will make any necessary adjustments to improve the picture in order that I may receive all the good that the Universe has for me now.

Since I am assured that my desires will be fulfilled according to the Love and Wisdom of my Supermind, my heart overflows with love and gratitude. The feeling of thankfulness pulsates throughout my entire being, and I am filled and thrilled with the joy of life. And it is so!

Keep the Power flowing. Once you've completed your treatment, it's time to move out into the world. . . and as you do, put the idea of success into action. You are going to *live* the idea, and through the living, the Power will be going before you to create new career opportunities for you and new success situations. *But you must get into the mainstream of activity.* You cannot sit back and wait for your good to "poof" in front of your eyes, but everything you do, do with ease, with poise and confidence, and with a more relaxed feeling. There is no stress or strain in your new program. A relaxed frame of mind keeps the power flowing smoothly through your Success Vibration, whereas an uptight feeling will restrict the flow—like putting pressure on a water hose will shut down the flow of water. More pressure, less water. Less pressure, more water. It's all the same principle.

It is suggested that you give yourself three treatments a day—morning, midday, and evening. Each treatment should be done with joy and enthusiasm, and last from 5 to 15 minutes. Once or twice a week, particularly on Saturday or Sunday, you may wish to spend more time in the visualizing stage to really get the feel of your fulfilled desires. Above all, don't make a treatment a chore—don't let it be something you feel pressure to do. To be effective, it must be done in a happy and peaceful frame of mind.

You must never forget that whatever you hold in consciousness as the truth about yourself and God will be mirrored in the world about you. If you think there is good and evil, there will be. If you think that God can withhold your good from you, it will be held back. If you think you can be sick, you will be. If you think you will fail, you will surely do so. If you think of yourself as just a "human being" subject to the winds of fate, you will ride that roller coaster all of your life, high one day and low the next, healthy and sick, plenty of money during "good" times and desperately in need of cash when times are "bad"—harmony followed by disorder, happiness and despair, peace and turmoil.

If you are having any kind of problem, do not condemn the situation or circumstance. Face yourself squarely in the mirror and acknowledge that you have been plugged into the race mind, which is nothing but the carnal consciousness of mankind, and declare that you have had enough of this mass illusion. Stake your claim to your inheritance, which is the Kingdom, and to the Truth of your being, which is the Spirit of God. Dedicate yourself to pulling the plug on mortal limitations and rising into a new consciousness of Power and Dominion.

The individuals who are realizing the Presence and Power of God within are saying, "I live in this world, but I am not of it. I do not accept anything but peace, power, and perfection—and this consciousness of the Ideal is outpictured in my world."

You can say the same thing. Identify yourself with Yourself and step out in mastery. Dare to rise above the sickness, lack, depression, discord, and unfulfillment of mortal human and become the Person you were created to be. Do it now. Every day you wait is a day delayed—and every day delayed puts you that much further behind in realizing the wonder and joy of life.

2

YOUR GIFTS AND
TALENTS FOR SUCCESS

Ask yourself, "What have I always wanted to do or be? What is my heart's desire? Where are my interests? What do I enjoy doing the most?" Spend several days contemplating these questions, and the answers will begin to flow into your mind. Go back to your childhood and come forward, remembering all those yearnings you've had. Write them down and see where the common denominator is. You'll find it. It may be something that you would discount or overlook because you could not see it as a means of supporting yourself in a job or career. Or it may be difficult for you to equate a particular heart's desire with a talent or gift.

For greater understanding of your gift and how

to use it, follow this exercise for seven days: Each morning, immediately upon awakening, ask yourself, "What do I intuitively feel my greatest strength to be? What do I intuitively feel my special gift or talent is?"

As you ask each question, write down the immediate thought that comes to mind. Ask the two questions and write down the answers. Once that is done, ask yourself one final question: "What do I intuitively feel my Higher Self wants me to do with these special attributes?" Again, put on paper the immediate response. Continue the process each day for seven days, not missing one single day. You will find that the answers for the first three days will be colored somewhat by your ego, but by the fourth day you will have broken through to a higher realm of consciousness, and the answers will pour forth with greater clarity.

What are some examples of gifts and talents? How about love, joy, and the ability to see something good in everything? Also think about wisdom and understanding, and the use of these gifts to help others move through a difficult time. Consider the ability to work with children in a variety of capacities, having a sense of humor and making others laugh, and the ability to create order out of chaos through proper organization. There are musical talents, using the voice, playing various instruments, and the ability to act and create a role so real that the audience loses all sense of time and space. Think about the ability to make something with your hands, capture beauty in a photograph, paint a picture, write a story or a poem, or teach someone—whether in a classroom or not.

There are so many additional gifts, and we have the potential to possess all of them—but certain ones are more pronounced in each individual consciousness. So find your gift—your talent—and polish it to perfection by using it to make this a better world.

Using your gifts and talents in a life program. Start writing your Life Program this very day. What do you want in life? I don't mean just making a list or a treasure map. Lists and maps are fine for the manifestation of things, but we're talking about a Life Program of *experiences* now, and the experiences will include the things. This is your opportunity to write the greatest drama ever written—and it will be for *you* because it will be the drama of *your* life. At the top of the page write: "I see myself..." and then write what you see from the standpoint of your highest vision. The choice is totally yours: What do you want to do and be and have? Drop all the can'ts, all the inhibitions. Put yourself at the center of your world, and build around you.

As you begin to write your scenario, the first thing should be how you see yourself spiritually. For example:

I see myself as a spiritual being, as the very Christ of God. I am so conscious of the Christ Self within that I have become that Self. I live and move and have my being in Christ, as Christ, and I am now the Master that I was created to be.

The second part of your script should be how you see the world, and the view of yourself living in the world:

I see myself living in a world of perfect peace and harmony, in a world filled with love and joy where the sense of separation from our Source is completely healed and humankind is now living as Godkind.

How about relationships?

I see myself in a beautiful, loving relationship; warm and tender, yet stimulating and exciting. I see perfect unconditional love in action between the two of us, and it is so wonderful. And I love the fun, the frolic, and the gaiety that I see in our relationship. We are so happy together.

Good health:

I see myself with a magnificently healthy body in perfect order, where every cell is in the image of the perfect pattern, and I am whole and complete.

Now look at your gifts and talents and see where you can find the deepest satisfaction in your life's work—whatever that may be. We're talking about your True Place now, where you see yourself doing what you've always wanted to do. And don't say you're too old or too young or too uneducated or too whatever. Throw away the excuses. Just write scenes showing yourself enjoying the greatest fulfillment of your eternal life—and don't be concerned with the financial part of it, or how you're going to make money doing what you really want to do. That's a separate part of your plan, so see yourself now doing what you have always wanted to do. Just write: "I see myself..." and write what you see.

Once this is complete, you can phase in the abundance of supply in your Life Program by seeing yourself as wealthy as you want to be:

I see myself financially independent and totally secure with lavish abundance.

Don't be concerned about where the money will come from—that's none of your business. Just see yourself overflowing with abundance and attracting bountiful prosperity from every direction, and write what you see.

Develop the other scenes of your life as you see ideal and perfect fulfillment, covering every desire, mastering every challenge, learning every lesson, capitalizing on every strength, using every gift and talent, and living life to the fullest. Don't worry about your writing style, your punctuation, or perhaps your inability to create vivid and dramatic scenes. You're not writing for publication—you are writing for *you*! If you want to make changes in the script later, that's fine because it's your Life Program. The main thing you want to do now is to

set the direction of your life accordin
est desires and your highest vision. I
we see ourselves, so we tend to becom

*I see myself energetic, inspired, and
enthusiastic. I see myself loving and loved,
unconditionally. I see myself poised, confident,
and filled with the power of absolute faith.
I see myself as whole and complete, with an
all-sufficiency of all things. I see myself with
perfect judgment and as Divine Wisdom in
action. I see myself as strong, mighty, and
powerful. I see myself as eternal Life in
perfect expression. I see myself joyous, happy,
and delighted to be me. I see myself enjoying
the Good Will of God every single day.
I see myself with perfect understanding.
I see myself as the Light of the world.
I see myself as God being me.*

Bringing your Life Program into visibility.
After you have written your Life Program in
detail—making sure that the scenes and visions
evoke great love, joy, and excitement—go to a
quiet place, sit up straight, and take several deep
breaths as you focus on the Love Center in your

...eart. Stir up that feeling of love until you feel its magnificent vibration, then read your Life Program to yourself with great feeling. Read the Program either silently or aloud, whichever way stirs up the greatest emotion in you. "I see myself..." Read it with overflowing love. "I see myself..." Read it with joyful tears. "I see myself..." Read it with power and strength. "I see myself..." Read it with great happiness. Read each word with feeling, and lovingly contemplate the scenes that come into your mind. Take as long as necessary to establish, register, and impress your deeper-than-conscious level of mind with the details of your Program.

Once you do this, you have the pattern, the mental equivalent, the mold for your Life Program—and it will remain etched in your consciousness unless you change the pattern. And this is why it is wise to read your Life Program each day until the manifestation occurs.

After the pattern is established, it is up to the power, the substance, and the creative energy of Spirit to give it form and experience. And while Infinite Mind is going to be the primary actor on stage now, you still have a vital role to play in the co-creation, as follows:

1. Remember who you are. The Reality of you is pure Spirit, the very Christ of God, the Lord-God-Self that you are in Truth.

2. Understand that the Life Program you create in your mind and write in words is not your conception. It is from your Higher Self; it is how your God-Self wants to express in your world. So you can relax, knowing that you don't have to make anything happen. All you have to do is take the blueprint into consciousness to establish the pattern.

3. The creative energy of that Infinite Mind within you is the substance of every form and experience of your Life Program. That radiant energy—that overflowing substance—is forever pouring, radiating from the Supermind within, right through your consciousness and out into the physical world to become all that you desire. As it moves through the pattern of your Life Program, the energy takes on the attributes of the program and begins to materialize them by changing its rate of vibration.

4. If you keep your focus on the *forms* of your Life Program, your mind will tell you after a time that there are not enough opportunities

to meet the right mate, not enough money to accomplish your goals, not enough contacts to find your true place, not enough physical well-being to meet your objectives, not enough time to do all that you want to do, not enough of whatever. And the reason is because your mind will be vibrating at too low a level; your mental vibrations will have dropped so low that the manifestation cannot be completed. This is why you must keep your mind on the spiritual I AM within, knowing that God is the very substance and activity of your Life Program. And since there is never any lack of substance of God or the activity of God, there cannot be any obstacles to the fulfillment of your Program.

In other words, there is always plenty of God! Saturate yourself with the idea of *plenty*, and the vibration of plenty will manifest in your affairs—plenty of love, plenty of health, plenty of true place opportunities, plenty of money, plenty of time, plenty of wisdom, plenty of fun, plenty of peace, plenty of joy, plenty of vitality, plenty of inspiration. PLENTY-PLENTY-PLENTY!

~ 3

REMOVING A MAJOR
OBSTACLE TO SUCCESS

One of the primary blocks in achieving true success can be summed up in the word *relationships*. Wherever there is any form of relationship, regardless of how casual or intense—whether with family, friends, associates in the workplace, even strangers—the law of cause and effect is in its most accelerated mode of action and reaction, casting a glaring light on the entire sowing and reaping process. With every action in thought, word, and deed, there is a compensating action, which becomes a cause for further action, which leads to additional reaction, and on and on throughout the universe.

This is the principle of "karma." Karmic causes did not come into play until the universe was thrown out of balance with the sense of separation—the dream of being separated from God and the formation of physical bodies. When the consciousness of unity and oneness of all life faded, the phenomenon of "relationships" came into being. The law of cause and effect became a part of the natural process at that time in order to restore universal equilibrium. It does this by bringing into balance through compensating factors every action for which we are responsible. On the outer scene we learn wisdom through experience; on the inner plane, perfection continues because the law has "thrown off" the discord to be harmonized in the universal karmic process.

In tracking these karmic effects through case histories of various individual situations, we see that in essentially every case of scarcity, sickness, accident, disappointment, failure, and unemployment, the faulty switch in the circuitry reflects a problem in one or more relationships—real or imagined. In each situation, physical, emotional, and mental energy was used to generate causes that threw things out of balance, resulting in a compensating force being returned to the sender.

Look at where you are in life at this moment.

You know that all the good in life is natural and automatic—that you have been given all that you could possibly desire for the most magnificent life imagined—yet you may be continuing to experience a shortage of supply, sickness in the body, unfulfillment in life, and other conditions that are contrary to the Divine Purpose and Standard. If you are, scan your consciousness to see and feel any relationship blips—husband, wife, son, daughter, father, mother, friends, acquaintances, associates (present and former), anyone and everyone on this side of the veil and beyond. A strong, hot, emotionally reactive blip tells you that you are generating a force that will ultimately return to you as some kind of an imbalance in your life. Even a faint, barely discernable echo may be the tip of the iceberg, with the great mass of judgment, condemnation, and resentment well below the surface. Yet it is still setting in motion a decree that you will eventually have to deal with.

Here are a few composite examples, summarized and simplified:

For years Frank experienced financial difficulties. Even with good money management he never had enough at any one time to meet his financial obligations. The energy involved here is the energy of supply, or abundance, and it was being screened out through discord in the family. Based on childhood memories of not being able to fully meet his mother's expectations, Frank grew up with a subconscious memory bank filled with feelings of being inept, incompetent, and ineffective. He projected these aspects of himself onto his wife and son and became severely critical of their "constant bungling"—resulting in a highly hostile home environment that produced even more guilt and anger. In time, Frank learned that the energy of abundance is the energy of love and goodwill. He also recognized that what he had been judging in others was what he was condemning in himself. Through love and forgiveness of that part of himself, he was able to find peace within and restore harmony in the home. It was not long before his consciousness opened to allow the supply to flow in its own natural way.

Doris was one of those (to use her words) "terribly unfulfilled" people who walk through life with head held low, and her daily chatter was about moving to another town to find greater happiness in life. What she did not realize at the time was that (1) we take our consciousness with us wherever we go, and (2) she was misusing the energy of divine order. This is the energy that produces joy in life and works naturally and automatically to express peace, poise, and confidence. How was the energy being diffused? By her constant criticism, put-down, and rejection of her husband, Tom. It was not until she learned that all husbands and wives are each other's "Shadow" did the healing process begin. The Shadow is our alter-ego representing everything about ourselves that we ever repressed, and our partner in life represents the Shadow's projection. What Doris was actually seeing in Tom was her masculine self as a complete bore—less spiritual than the feminine, unenlightened, naive, and an unworthy companion in life. Once she understood that side of herself, made peace with it, and withdrew the projections from Tom, she found a new sense of joy in life. The fulfillment that she was seeking came *naturally* through a new career opportunity, stimulating new friends, and a renewed love affair with Tom.

Wayne had spent most of his adult life either unemployed or underemployed, never seeming to get into the groove of "right livelihood." Obviously the energy of success was being shut down. In tracing this to a possible relationship problem, Wayne finally realized that he was very apathetic regarding intimate family relationships, and that he carried this attitude even further as far as friends were concerned. He admitted that his life was almost completely self-oriented, that he was satisfied without interaction with others, and was not inspired to develop close personal relationships—except with some people who lived at a distance (no sudden invasion of privacy). At the root of a lethargic, self-satisfied mind that opposes the cultivation of right relations is a fear of being dominated by others, which blocks energy that naturally expresses as achievement, advancement, good fortune, and happy outcomes. Wayne has now begun to appreciate what true family bonding means, and he's also starting to reach out to others in his community—striving to develop and maintain real and lasting friendships. As the energy of success is released, whole new fields of opportunity will open to him, including his True Place in life.

The Power Plant within. From the Blazing Sun of Love within, the all-inclusive Rays shine forth to express the Unlimited All-Good. It is our Self fulfilling Itself through us, and our consciousness is the acceptor, the transformer, and, yes, the limiter. Our Loving Holiness says, "All that I have is yours, and I am eternally giving all that I am to you." How much can we accept? By our own decisions, how much of the finished kingdom will be transformed into incompleteness? How many limitations must we place on the infinite givingness?

It is absolutely true that the Spirit of the Essential Self will help to clear Its channel of expression through the energy of forgiveness and love, and without a doubt all karmic debts can be dissolved by a sufficient rise in consciousness. But we will not be open to that love and cannot reverse the laws of mental and emotional gravity until we take the necessary steps in this world to clean up our mess. This was spelled out very clearly in John 5:17—"My Father is working still, and I am working." It must be a cooperative effort of conscious mind and Master Self working together. Through our attunement with Self we can be guided every step of the way. We can be shown the hot spots in every relationship and how we "relate" to (meaning interaction with) God, Self, our own personality, people in general, and every kind of person who comes into the range of our consciousness. We can be taken into the past to see where we initiated karmic causes, and on the screen of our mind we can view every situation where we cast true or false bread upon the waters of life. But the decision to become totally involved in this healing process is ours, and we must take the initiative to follow through with action.

Since the energy involved in relationships is the stuff that resistance is made of, it seems to me that a top priority would be to get ourselves clear and clean. Make a list of everyone who could possibly trigger even a trace of irritation. Look at the anger, the hurt, the disappointment, the resentment, the judgment—and understand that you are condemning yourself. Then isolate that disliked part of yourself that you have projected on others and take it into the Light of Spirit to be loved, forgiven, and healed. This enables you to give up resentment toward everyone (the meaning of forgiveness) and restore harmony in your world. And if you are led to take a specific action on the physical plane in a one-on-one encounter to further harmonize the situation, do it.

Remember that you are not trying to create, change, or improve anything in the physical world; you are not trying to get something that is not already there. All that you are attempting to do is get into the flow of the natural process—and do what comes naturally.

4

THE LAW OF SUCCESS WORKS ON MANY LEVELS

The power of God meets us on whatever level of consciousness we may be experiencing at the time. Think about that. Perhaps another way of saying the same thing is that our world is always a reflection of how we think and feel. That's the way the Law works. To give you a clearer understanding of the principle involved, we'll look at a few illustrations.

Let's say that you are a pure materialist and the only priority in your life is a material or physical goal. Whether it is to earn a certain sum of money, land a job, reach the top rung of the corporate ladder, find a mate, or to have "security" in later years, your entire focus is on the planning and the implementation of the plan to achieve the goal. There must always be a third-dimensional "target" to shoot at, and the target will marshal the physical-mental forces of consciousness and direct your energy toward that desire fulfillment.

Does God work with you on this level? Certainly! But the power will work with you, and for you, only as it works *as* you. In other words, if meeting your objectives on this level requires that you ignore everything else in life and become a workaholic, then the power working *as* your consciousness will assume that role and you will burn a lot of midnight oil. With that one-pointed focus of the goal/objective in mind, you will acquire all the know-how you can; you'll learn all the techniques in "playing to win"—and you'll work with personal will power to achieve your goal regardless of the consequences.

You will learn how to cope with fear through aggressive action, and your self-image will develop into a mental picture of yourself as a shrewd, tough, decisive go-getter. And while stress and tension may affect the physical system, there are always good doctors to fix you up and send you back on the road to success. If a marriage dissolves through the tunnel vision of this type of consciousness, so be it. There are always others out there who will appreciate you.

Yes, the impersonal power of God does meet you on this level, appearing as the dedication required to achieve the goal, the stamina to stay with it, the medicine to ease your pain, and the attracting force to bring people into your life with a similar vibration in consciousness—positive or negative. What about heartfelt prayers? A fervent, persistent prayer spoken from this consciousness is always answered, with the fullness of the deliverance dependent upon the measure of "blind" faith set in motion. "It is done unto you as you believe."

I don't want to give the impression that people on this level cannot be happy. They can, but their happiness is usually measured by how close they are to achieving their goals, and the carrot must forever be on the end of the stick.

The discovery of the genie. As the materialist achieves one goal after another (or seemingly so) and sets up new targets, new objectives, there may come a time when a sense of dissatisfaction creeps into consciousness and the questions start. "What is all this for? Why isn't there more happiness in my life? What can I do to find greater peace of mind?" After a while this nagging feeling may lead the person to the discovery of Truth ideas—perhaps from a book or through the sharing of another individual. The intellectual interest is stirred, and the exciting mystery of the subconscious mind begins to capture his or her imagination. This person reads or hears that affirmations can "make things happen" and much emphasis is placed on mind power. The holy servant has been found, and the individual is determined to use this servant to find the missing peace and happiness. After all, when you've found the secret of mind over matter, you can let the genie of the mind do the work, But genies can also make you think you are more evolved than you are. Let me give you an example.

The great metaphysician Emmet Fox wrote about a young child who had just fallen off a bridge into the water below. He pointed out that if you are spiritually evolved, you can just stand there on the bridge and "see" the child safely on the shore, and lo and behold, the child *is* safely on shore. But if you are not in an evolved state of consciousness, you don't stand around waiting for something to happen. Fox suggests that you quickly dive off the bridge into the water—praying all the way—and save the child.

I have found that many of the "third-dimensionals" who are introduced to New Thought try to demonstrate while still operating out of lower mind and power, and the result is a lot of "drowning." One man I know would certainly match the description of a wheeler-dealer. When he discovered metaphysics, he decided that "make-it-happen" affirmations would unleash the genie to wheel and deal for him and he wouldn't have to work so hard. His demonstration was the loss of his job. He had been out of work for about six months (and affirming daily that a new position was being attracted to him) when he called me. The gist of the conversation was that his prayers were not working and he needed some help. After a few minutes I asked, "Why don't you go find a job?" And he replied, "Because I want to do it God's way." (To him, "God" was simply a force in his subconscious that was amenable to control by the power of suggestion.)

After discussing the concept of the one Presence and Power, universal and individualized, I said something along these lines: "God always meets us on the level of our consciousness. You are out of work, and you want a job. Right now, God sees you as totally fulfilled and enjoying creative self-expression in your true place, but the vibration of your consciousness is not strong enough for this Divine Ideal to express perfectly. So while you're continuing to work to uplift and expand consciousness, go out and look for a job, affirming all the time that God is with you, directing your every move." He followed these instructions and quickly found an excellent job.

Just remember that when your consciousness is more material than spiritual, you may find your answer through specific activity on the material plane; that is, diving off the bridge, reviewing the want ads, working with the law of averages in making sales calls, et cetera. And as you combine these physical-mental activities with spiritual work to expand consciousness, you will find your feeling nature coming into play.

Emotions become the fuel for the next phase of consciousness. When my wife, Jan, and I first discovered Truth concepts, we were living in the Chicago area in the 1960s. We have been functioning in a "physical-mental" consciousness most of our lives, but when we were exposed to Truth, it didn't take long to activate our emotional system. Perhaps it was the excitement and enthusiasm we felt...it was as though we had always known the metaphysical principles, and the "remembering" was a great stimulus to our feeling nature.

We soon made a list of 20 things, experiences, and conditions we wanted, and we went to work. We began every morning by reviewing our list, imagined that we had the fulfillment of each desire, affirmed that it was so, and spoke the word that it was done. And soon everything on that list came to pass—and so we made new and bigger and better lists with demonstrations following. But before we could completely conquer our world, everything fell apart like a sawdust doll.

We realized later that we had been operating strictly on mind power (conscious/subconscious), and I can assure you that there is a missing ingredient when you are working only with third-dimensional forces. Even though we had united the mental, emotional, and physical energies, we were still operating on the plane of the lower self, or personality. We had not yet tuned into that Christ Vibration within, the Superconsciousness. We forgot Jesus' instructions to seek the kingdom first.

You may ask, "Did God meet you on that integrated level of personality consciousness?" Yes, indeed! As we began to choose exactly what we wanted in life and developed the consciousness for those choices, they appeared in our lives. But here was the snag: We were developing a consciousness of things, material conditions, and physical experiences, rather than a consciousness of God. And the things, conditions, and experiences were only as permanent in the outer world as our ability to constantly project them. It was like having a tire with a slow leak—we constantly had to pump it up.

In essence, the new "world" that we had projected for ourselves required constant attention and mind-management through affirmations and treatments, and day after day our attention was placed on drilling the mind and programming consciousness. We felt that we couldn't leave the "projection booth" for one moment, but obviously we did—and the screen went blank. We just couldn't hold the picture anymore, but in the divine scheme of things, that was the best thing that ever happened to us because it forced us to surrender and let everything go.

Becoming spiritually centered. When you're back at the bottom of the mountain, there is only one place to go, and that's up—and so we started the climb again, this time with a total dedication to the

Spirit within. And as we began to reshape and retune consciousness, we were very gently led by Spirit to redirect the focus of our affirmations, treatments, and meditations. Whereas before we had been working to demonstrate a better "outer" condition, we began to use these tools to demonstrate the Love and Power of God. I'm not saying that we no longer had any desires, plans, or visions of a totally fulfilled life. Hardly. In fact, the scenario of our Life Plan expanded even more as we glimpsed what was included in the Father's storehouse. But there was a total redirection in our spiritual work.

For example, all former prosperity treatments were directed to the phenomenal world, as if to *make* more money appear in the bank, or create conditions whereby new clients would appear and new cars and houses would manifest. Health treatments were directed to the body, relationship treatments were aimed at the particular individuals, and protection treatments were focused on unseen, negative forces "out there" somewhere. The whole focus of mind and emotions was *outer* directed.

Then one day, without really realizing what we were doing, we began to affirm, treat, and meditate for the sole purpose of awakening consciousness. We were becoming spiritually centered, and with this change in direction came the knowledge that the only real and lasting demonstration is the demonstration of the Truth of Being. So instead of constantly affirming prosperity, we began to affirm our oneness with the Source of Abundance right within us that has no conception whatsoever of lack. And in our spiritual treatments we began by tuning into the Christ Vibration first and continued from the standpoint that it was our Christ Self doing the treating—and since Spirit knows only life, love, order, harmony, perfection, and nothing to the contrary, no obstacles or barriers loomed up to block our vision. And in our meditations we devoted our time to contemplating the Christ Presence, the indwelling Spirit, knowing that this True Self would awaken the subconscious from within— rather than it being programmed from without.

Things didn't completely turn around overnight, but as the changes began to occur, even the small ones were very meaningful. And soon the momentum picked up, and our lives began to change dramatically with greater prosperity, beautiful health, and more loving relationships than we had ever known. You see, when God meets you on the spiritual level of consciousness, it's the Real Thing. The "effect" is lasting, the fulfillment joyous, and there is the constant emotion of gratitude.

A few realizations along the way:

Prayer is the opening of consciousness to God, providing a door for Spirit to enter the third-dimensional plane. While God is omnipresent, the activity of God cannot take place in your experience except through a spiritual consciousness.

"I and the Father are one." This is true in the absolute, but it is not true in your experience until you realize it.

Prayer is not trying to convince God to do something for you. It is becoming aware of the Presence within you, knowing that God acts for your highest good through this conscious awareness.

The Father has given you the kingdom. It's already yours, and everything you could possibly desire in life is in the kingdom. When you love enough, the kingdom radiates out through the door that love has opened.

Abundance is yours now. You would not be alive in this world if this were not true. The life force and the energy of supply are the same. Recognize your Source and let the living abundance pour forth into your experience.

Disease, illness, and ailments are effects, simply "appearances." If you judge such an appearance as bad, you bind it in your experience. Withhold judgment and let the Presence correct the appearance.

There is nothing that your Christ Self cannot do for you. In fact, It is doing everything for you now. Relax.

You don't "own" anything. Everything is an expression and extension of the Presence within you, so all belongs to Spirit. Remember, "the earth is the Lord's, and the fullness thereof."

Whatever you resist you give energy to. Whatever you give energy to continues to be a part of your experience. If you want a so-called evil out of your life, stop resisting it. When you pull the plug on its power, it dies out of your experience.

If you believe in good and evil, you have created a second power out of your own energy, and you will experience that evil because it is in your consciousness. When you realize Omnipotence, the one and only Power, then only the Power of Good is at work in your life.

Don't put your faith in anything visible, either "good" or "evil." That which appears good may not be, and to fear an evil (put your faith in it) will only sustain it. Place your faith only in the invisible Presence and Power within you.

You don't need to tell others how spiritual you are. They already know "by your fruits." Your health, harmony, peace, joy, and fulfillment are in direct proportion to the level of your spirituality.

You are not here to live a passive life. The Universe needs you.

The only problem facing you in life is the belief in separation from your Source. Solve that one, and all the others will vanish.

Before you look for "new" Truths, put into practice those you already know.

Everyone in your life is there by the Law of Attraction. And whether you consider them good, bad, or indifferent, they are there to help you experience your self.

If you feel a negative emotion about a personality characteristic in another person, chances are you have that same flaw in your consciousness, otherwise you could not see it in others.

5

YOUR TRUE WORTH

The Universe does not compensate individuals based on the activity of work, but on the activity of consciousness. Accordingly, if you feel that your life is empty and useless—that your work is insignificant—and that the things that are yours to do are really meaningless, then you will be pressing out of universal Substance an income directly related to that consciousness: insignificant, trivial, useless, and valueless. On the other hand, once you see yourself as you are in truth, and embody that vision in your feeling nature, you will move above lack and limitation.

You are an heir to all that the Father has, and all you have to do to receive your inheritance is to die to your old ways of thinking. Rising in place will be the Truth of you—a strong, vibrant, useful, significant, valuable, worthwhile, meaningful, loving, and fulfilled individual.

Begin now to love those empty places in your life FULLY. Get to really know yourself, and love that rediscovered you with everything you've got. Then look at every detail of your home and work life and let the love flow. Nothing is too insignificant for the Energy of Love, so be a radiating Center of Love wherever you are.

A Meditation

I came into this world with a very specific purpose.
I came to fulfill a mission.
I came to love life and realize the truth about me.
I came to contribute to the salvation of this world.

I am part of God and the fullness of the
Godhead dwells in me.
In the Mind of God, no one, or no thing
is useless or meaningless.
Everyone and everything is of critical importance
to the balance and order of the universe.
Without me, God would not be complete.
Without me, the universe would lose
its equilibrium.

All that is before me to do,
I do with happy enthusiasm.
For nothing is too insignificant.
And never again will there be a sense
of futility in my life.

I am overflowing with gratitude to the Father for
the opportunity to be in physical form at this time.
I am so thankful to be right where I am, right now,
serving all who come my way with love,
joy, understanding, and forgiveness.

Recognizing my true worth,
I now go forth with uplifted vision.
I see with the inner eye the loving and
prospering activity of the Christ within.
I see with my physical eyes
lavish abundance everywhere.
I am peaceful, powerful, and poised,
for I know who I am.

6

SELECTED EXCERPTS ON THE ATTRIBUTES OF SUCCESS

Consciousness—The Right Vibration

Early in my spiritual journey I became aware that every problem I encountered was simply an outpicturing of my consciousness. Accordingly, I began to study the makeup of consciousness and meditate on its meaning—and over a period of time a new understanding of this principle of life was developed. For example:

It is my consciousness, and not the consciousness of others, that shapes my life and molds my world.

Every single experience in my life, whether "good" or "bad," is created out of the vibration of my consciousness. The higher the vibration, the greater the degree of Good in my life.

I do not work to develop a healthier body. Rather, I work to gain a consciousness of health, a spiritual consciousness of wholeness.

If I dwell on limitation and insufficiency in any area of my life, I am building a consciousness of lack, and lack always attracts more lack.

If I say "I can't afford" something, I am building a "can't afford" consciousness, and the law will bring more things and experiences into my life that I can't afford.

In demonstrating an all-sufficiency in my life, I seek the realization that my consciousness of God AS my supply IS my supply.

If I worry about what others are saying and doing, I am giving my energy to a so-called outside power—which emphasizes the belief in duality and keeps me anchored in the third dimension.

I cannot judge the actions of others, because they cannot help doing what they are doing. They are simply operating out of their present sense of identity, a particular level of consciousness.

If I am uptight, heavy, concerned, or anxious about anyone, I am becoming negatively attached to that person, which gives him/her power over me. I cut the cord on anyone who makes me feel less than I am in truth.

When I expect anything from anyone, I am setting myself up to be let down. But when my expectations are directed toward Spirit, I am never disappointed. I place my faith in God and only God.

Every person in my life is there by right of consciousness. Whether they are constructive or destructive, they are in my life through the Law of Attraction.

If I look outside for my good, I am deserting my Source and closing the channel (in my consciousness) to the flow of blessings.

*When I think of myself as not in my true place,
consciousness will make sure that I am not.
But when I realize that Spirit is never out of
place, and I am that Spirit, the true place that
always was is revealed.*

Everything comes to you or is repelled from you based on the vibration of your energy field, and the vibration is established by your beliefs and convictions. Accordingly, you can see that nothing is out of place or out of order in your life. Everything is perfect based on your consciousness and the outworking of the law. Your world is a mirror of your thoughts, feelings, and concepts—all pressed out in material form and experience.

Do you like what you see? You are the architect and the builder, and you have designed and produced your world to the exact specifications of your consciousness.

To run around trying to fix your world with the consciousness that produced the problem in the first place will only aggravate the situation even more. To change your world you must change your consciousness. You must draw forth from within a new awareness, understanding, and knowledge of the universe, the power that sustains you, and the true nature of yourself. And with each degree in the shift in your consciousness, more Reality is revealed in your world.

Creative Intelligence

See the energy of Creative Intelligence as a soft light expanding in your head, then moving down to your heart, on down to your solar plexus, radiating down your body and out all around you. Once you are centered in the light, speak these words with great feeling:

I see. I understand. I know. I AM.
I mentally see the Truth within every so-called
problem. I intuitively see the Reality behind
every illusion. I thoughtfully see through every
obstacle. I understand the Principle of Being.
I know the absoluteness of the Law. I AM
a spiritual being and I am free to BE
according to my highest vision.

There is great clarity in my consciousness now as I view that which is before me to do. As a creator with God, I conceive and extend only the true thought-forms of wholeness, harmony, and abundance. I see myself living in a world of perfect peace, in a world filled with love and joy where the sense of separation from the Source is completely healed.

In my creative imagination I see myself as whole and healed, with an all-sufficiency of all things at all times. I see myself as loved and loving, unconditionally. I see myself as joyous, happy, and delighted to be me. I am on course now—poised, secure, and confident in the Light of Creative Intelligence.

Faith

Faith is your consciousness. You think, feel, speak, and act according to your consciousness, according to your faith. Faith is the substance (the creative energy) of things hoped for, the evidence of things unseen; therefore, your consciousness is that which stands under and supports (the substance of) what you are experiencing in your world.

If your consciousness is filled with fear and anxiety, that is where your faith is. You are putting your faith in the possibility and probability of misfortune, lack, and limitation. Your consciousness, which is your faith, your substance, must by law act upon itself.

Your faith vibration attracts what you have and experience in this world because like must attract like! Where is your faith? Look around you. If your faith is on all-sufficiency, then so it is in your life. If your faith is pulsating to a "just getting by" frequency, then so it is in your world. If your faith is on the dial-set of insufficiency, then there will never be enough to meet your needs.

The faculty of DIVINE FAITH (faith energy pulsating according to its divine vibration) may represent only a tiny particle of light within your lower mind at the present time. But Jesus said that if your faith was no larger than a grain of mustard seed (or just a faint glow of light), you could level a mountain. And you ask: "What about that mountain of debt, this peak of despair in my relationships, that volcano that has erupted in my body, those rising fears regarding my career?" Could the answer be that you have not recognized this Power Center as being an integral part of your individualized cosmic system? Could it simply be that you are not aware that you have this inexhaustible Power right at your disposal?

When we become aware of our Power of Faith, the energy from that Center begins to work for us according to the Divine Standard, the original High Vibration.

Contemplate these statements:

I believe there is NOTHING God cannot do. I believe there is nothing God cannot do THROUGH me. I believe there is nothing God cannot do AS me. God is my Self; therefore, there is nothing that I cannot do. Nothing is too good for God, and nothing is too good for me!

I love the Faith I AM with all my heart, and I now draw forth the omnipotence of this incredible energy and command it to fill my feeling nature with its Power. Come forth, my Faith! Saturate my emotions with total trust, total certainty, total conviction in myself as a being of God. I AM Substance. I AM Creative Energy.

*I AM God being me now. Through the pure
Energy of Faith, I feel the Truth!*

Gratitude

Always remember that your desires are first fulfilled in consciousness, and then they come forth in the outer world clothed with materiality—so the secret is to be thankful while your good is still invisible. You can't wait until you possess the visible form to express your gratitude or you will delay the entire process, or cancel it out altogether.

Gratitude releases a dynamic current of spiritual energy to go before you to exert a mighty influence in your world. It not only eliminates negative patterns in the subconscious caused by ingratitude, it also forms a connecting link—a bridge—between you and every possible source of good in your life. Of course, there is only one Source, but Divine Mind works in mysterious ways to perform magnificent wonders through an infinite number of channels. And through a feeling of gratitude and praise for the Master Consciousness within, you put yourself in alignment with all of the riches of the universe.

Unconditional Love

To be a co-creator with the Spirit of Love, you must think love, feel love, speak love, and act with love. Your first thought of love should be to respond to the love that your God-Self is eternally pouring out upon you. Since this Presence within you loves you with all of Its Divine Consciousness, should you not reciprocate by loving this Reality of you will all your mind, your heart, and your strength? Can you not express gratitude for that love by returning the love in full measure? When you do, the Connection is restored, and the middle wall of partition is blown away.

Speak these words with passion:

God loves me. God loves me!
Regardless of any mistake I have ever
made, the Creator of Life loves me with all of
Its Being. And since God loves me, how could
I possibly not love myself?

*Oh [state your name], I love you so! I love this
me that is, the I that I AM, this self, this person,
this mind, this spirit. My God! I am talking about
You! When I love myself, I am loving You! And
when I love You, I am loving myself, for we are
eternally One. What a glorious Truth!*

*Now that I am aware again that Love is the
Reality behind all form, I cannot love anything
without loving everything, and so I do. I love
everyone and everything everywhere. There are no
conditions to this love, no qualifications. I am in
love, and love is in me, and I let the glorious Love
Energy pour through me now to heal every relationship and harmonize every situation in my life.*

*I am a radiating center of Divine Love. I feel it.
I know it. I AM it! I now go forth into the world
as the incredible Energy of Love!*

To keep you on course during the day, use this
short affirmation:

*I work lovingly and easily for God, and my life is
filled with wholeness, harmony, and abundance.*

Will

Will is the directive power of consciousness and is closely linked with choice, decision, and decree. When the will is focused on spiritual ideals, you are moving toward the Christ Connection. And as you are willing to "be about the Father's business," you are reconnecting the purpose of the lower nature with the Will of the Higher Self, and this true I AM can then express the fullness of Its potentiality in and through your consciousness.

Watch what happens in your energy field when you speak these declarations with power:

I am determined to be all that I was created to be!
I choose to express the fullness of my Christhood!
I now make a conscious decision to step
out into mastery in this lifetime!
I decree a full awakening to the Christ within!
I now link my will with the Will of my Higher Self
and move forward to fulfill my mission and
purpose in this incarnation!
I achieve my destiny!
I fulfill my mission!

Do you sense the power, the determination, the feeling of commitment? This is the consciousness of the Spiritual Warrior where nothing is impossible! The will faculty, which is located in your energy field near the front center of the brain, is now glowing with radiant light, and like steam in a boiler, its force will propel you toward your destination—literally rolling over every seeming obstacle. But without the balancing effect of love, will can be a power out of control, with the "end justifying the means" becoming the primary motivation.

Think of it this way: In the Mind of God, "will" means the Cosmic Urge to express, and that expression is always with and in love, meaning the highest Good-for-all. Your will is your urge to express the fullness of your potentiality, but the radiating force must be controlled by unconditional love. Mind and emotions, head and heart, must be united in and for *Goodwill*.

If you ever wake up in the morning feeling listless and uninspired, or if life seems to have no meaning for you and there is little motivation to move toward a goal, or if you find yourself floundering around with little self-discipline, then you need a good shot of the Power Energy of Will and Purpose. In your imagination see a switch-plate marked **Energy of Will and Purpose**. Notice that the switch is in the OFF position. See yourself flipping the switch to ON and "hear" the sound deep within you—a hum similar to a generator starting up. Mentally connect with the radiating energy and feel the vibration. While you are using your imagination to activate the energy flow, this is not an imaginary exercise. The imaging-feeling action is literally directing the flow of energy through your system. Once you feel the radiation, speak these words with great enthusiasm:

The Power of God is working mightily in me now. I am hooked up to the Dynamo within, and I am electrified with the Divine Energy of Will and Purpose. I am quickened from head to toe, galvanized into action by the invincible currents flowing in and through me.

I am stirred, excited, and thrilled over the opportunity this day to be and do and have according to the unlimited Vision of the Master Self I AM.

I no longer stand in my way, for I am God in expression, and God does not have obstacles or obstructions. My consciousness is on fire with will and purpose, and I am fired up!

I now go forth to joyfully accomplish my mission.

Wisdom

Remember that it is not your ego who is all-wise. As Socrates wrote: "The Delphic oracle said I was the wisest of all the Greeks. It is because I alone, of all the Greeks, know that I know nothing." And this is true of you, but when your Wisdom faculty is awakened, your consciousness becomes the channel through which the Wisdom, Understanding, and Knowledge of the Omniscient Christ Mind flows.

Spiritual treatment for wisdom:

I am the Power of Wisdom, and I call on this Power now to fill my heart and mind with the Light of perfect judgment and intuition. Through Christ in me, the very spirit of God I AM, my actions are right and perfect. I know what to do at all times and in every situation. And I always do the right thing because it is the right thing to do! I know! I feel! And what I know and what I feel are Spiritual Knowledge and Inspiration are guiding me every step of the way. God cannot make mistakes, and neither can I when I am consciously aware of the Presence within. I am now aware of that Presence, and I am filled and thrilled with the Illumination of Spirit.
I AM Wisdom!

7

A MASTER PLAN
FOR SUCCESS

Those of you who have worked with the energies of the "60-day nonhuman program" as discussed in my book *A Spiritual Philosophy for the New World,* know that it is a process that truly produces miracles. The reason: We give up our mortal sense of existence with its concepts of life and death, good and evil, rich and poor, success and failure, wellness and illness, peace and war, and love and hate. We let it all go, wave good-bye to a human sense of being, and begin our journey into the Fourth Dimension as "Nonhumans."

We do this by recognizing that on the human level we will never get out of the revolving door, and by acknowledging the greatest spiritual secret in this world: *"I of myself can do nothing."* This is not resignation; this is POWER THINKING. As the Ageless Wisdom stated it, and later echoed by Paul, "Have nothing and you possess everything."

Why 60 days and not 40, as in my audiocassette *The 40-Day Prosperity Plan*? That plan deals with a particular energy that becomes visible as money. Success, however, means different things to different people and usually relates to some form of achievement. Thus, there are more factors involved—such as goals, a contribution or service to be made, creative activity, interaction with people, planning, right timing, decisions to make, discernment, and tenacity. In demonstrating Spirit as the Source of our supply, the mind realizes Cause, and Cause becomes effect, a direct-line proposition. But in dealing with the idea of success, I feel that more time should be given to the "packaging"—the coming together—of all the elements involved in the achievement process. It could possibly be done in 10, 20, or 30 days, but let's follow a 60-day program to release the living energy of success and fully demonstrate Spirit as that which we call happy outcomes, victory, attainment, affluence.

An Adaptation of the 60-Day Program Specifically for True-Place Success

Step 1: Write down what you would consider complete success in your life and affairs—your ideas of good fortune, triumph, and fulfillment. Read it over, then place the paper in an envelope, seal it, and put it in a drawer—not to be seen again for 60 days.

Step 2: On another piece of paper, write the following statement: "I am willing to give up my personal concepts of success in favor of my Divine Self's purpose for my true-place success in this lifetime."

Understand that the personal mind does not have the wisdom, vision, or power to know, see, and accomplish the *ultimate* in successful living. But the Divine Consciousness does—and Its intentions are so much greater and grander than anything we could possibly imagine. By letting the Self's purpose be fulfilled, our lives are transformed into a state of bliss unknown to personal consciousness. You see, the Omnipotent One within sees no obstacles, knows no obstructions, has no "sense" of delay, recognizes no opposing power.

There *is* a Divine Plan for each one of us, and

as we surrender to the Master within totally and completely, that Plan moves into the implementation stage. The inner Guidance will show us exactly what to do to "get into position" with carefully defined steps to take. And the Law of Attraction will become a mighty force to bring people, situations, and experiences into our lives to accelerate the fulfillment process. The Law doesn't think about the excuses we might conjure up to hinder true success—such as age, education, lack of money, the state of the economy, or world conditions. It sees only *fulfillment.*

Step 3: Establish the date that you will start the program, and mark the calendar to show the duration of the two-month period. A few days before you begin the program write an Agreement with your God-Self, the Holy "I" within. The purpose of the Agreement is to surrender everything that relates to your human sense of being to your Master Self. Make the statement that you are willing to give up everything on the third-dimensional plane in order to have everything Fourth Dimensionally.

When I say "give up," I am not talking about removing everything and everyone *physically.* The giving up, the releasing, the surrendering all takes place in consciousness—where it counts most. Put your statement in writing and leave nothing out. Give up your body, your emotions, your mind. Surrender your family, friends, bank account, debts, bills—all your possessions—everything that you own in this world. The objective is to become totally detached and impersonal to your material sense of existence.

Then add to your list all your fears, needs, wants, desires, judgments, resentments, unforgiveness, jealousy, dislikes, and hates. Be specific, name names, spell it out! Finally, include all positions that you have taken for or against anything or anyone, and all causes and convictions about which you feel emotional. This is an inventory of all you are and have as a human being, so keep working with the list until it is complete—*hold nothing back.*

Step 4: Your participation in this Program does not mean that you will just "sit" for 60 days and neglect your responsibilities in the physical world. You will continue your life as before, but you will be operating on a different vibration in consciousness; you will be focusing on *spirituality* rather than *materiality*, and all action you take in the outer world will be spirit directed.

Do not pray for any material form or experience during the 60-day period. All meditation during this period must only be for deeper realization of who and what you are. Agree that for 60 days your conscious mind will assume the primary role as a silent witness to the Activity of Spirit. If any desires, needs, wants, or wishes come into your mind, release them quickly with the words *"I have surrendered everything to Spirit. For 60 days I am only going to serve Spirit and not my ego. I now release the pull in my consciousness to the Christ within to be transmuted."*

If you are tempted to demonstrate money or a job, speak the words: *"I of myself can do nothing. The Spirit of God within me does the work, and Spirit is doing and being everything now. My only responsibility in this matter is to abide in Spirit."*

To make this program work, you must give up concern about anything and everything, knowing that through your awareness of the indwelling Presence all things within the range of your consciousness are adjusted, harmonized, healed, prospered, and protected. And when emotional charges are set off in your system and "Oh-Lord-what-will-I-do?" thoughts come into your mind, just stop right there and say:

This is none of my business. Those red flags were for my human self, and it does not exist anymore. I am a spiritual being living in a spiritual universe as a witness to the Activity of God, and I refuse to descend back into the dense vibrations to fight the battle. I've given everything to Spirit, and now I have everything spiritually—and this spiritual energy is now revealing the Finished Kingdom. I am free at last!

Step 5: Begin each day, even before you get out of bed, by expressing loving gratitude for all the good in your life, for the everywhere present Activity of God. Even the most destitute and desperate can always find something to be thankful about, and this you must do for it is of critical importance. By daily "counting your blessings," a vibration of love and joy will begin to move through your consciousness calling for all the good in your life to grow and multiply.

If you will truly dedicate yourself to living as a *spiritual being* for the full 60 days, you just might wake up one morning and find that you are living in the Fourth Dimension—where everything you could possibly desire is already in perfect expression as form and experience.

The Daily Plan

To help you stay on track, I have given you 30 days of thoughts, with a brief explanation behind each idea. At the end of the 30-day period, start over, and watch how your consciousness expands during the second cycle.

Spend at least five minutes contemplating the idea, going beyond the words to the true essence, and let it become a vital point of your consciousness for the day. Immediately follow this with a focused meditation on your Divine Self. Ponder the Infinite Knowingness of that Self—Its Wisdom and Intelligence. Meditate on Its Life, Love, Joy, and Power. Feel and sense the incredibly creative energy radiating from the Infinite Mind within and focus on what this energy represents. Be aware that it is the very Thought Energy of God, embodying perfect Thought-forms of abundance, wholeness, harmony, protection, peace, right relations, right actions, divine order, divine guidance, and the substance of all physical forms and experiences. Then, "sink into Spirit" and *listen* to the voice within.

It would be helpful if you kept a journal during the 60 days and recorded your thoughts, feelings, and new experiences in consciousness and in the outer world of form. Above all, be prepared for positive change in your life.

Thoughts to Ponder Throughout Each Day

DAY 1

I of myself can do nothing. It is the Spirit within who expresses and manifests as true success in my life.

What does a human being think about most of the time? Lack, limitation, unfulfillment, disease, disorder, death, the possibility of this and the probability of that, the law of averages, and on and on. All of these ideas blend into one of self-identification because the human identifies all of these ideas with his or her own experience. But what happens when I fully commit to the idea that "I of myself can do nothing"? The mind shifts to encompass that which can do *something*, for the universe cannot tolerate inaction. The mind seeks a power, the presence of authority, to take the place of the I that can do nothing. That presence is the Spirit within, my true Self.

DAY 2

*I have surrendered everything in my life
to the Spirit of God within.*

I have made the commitment to become totally detached to lack, debt, ailments, possessions,
conditions, and situations in my individual world.
I have cut the cord on people, places, and things
that caused pulls in my consciousness; and I put
my emotions under control of my Higher Self so
that all resentment, condemnation, judgment,
unforgiveness, and jealousy will be transmuted.

DAY 3

This day I serve Spirit and not my ego.

I know that I created my ego with my fears—
but my ego has no power except that which I give
it, and it has been taken away. Now I look only to
the Spirit within, my Holy Self, as the only Source,
Cause, and Power in my life—and I serve my
Spirit through this loving awareness of Its
Presence and by faithfully following the guidance
from within.

DAY 4

I dwelleth in the secret place of the Most High;
I abide under the shadow of the Almighty.

I now live in Spirit—in spiritual consciousness—and I am protected, guided, and guarded every moment. There truly is nothing to fear in Omnipotence.

DAY 5

Instead of praying for things and conditions,
I ponder the invisible Allness that is
already mine within.

I have everything now, for I have been given the Kingdom. There is nothing missing in my life, and I let the fullness of the Kingdom come forth now into perfect expression.

DAY 6

*My identity as a human being has created
human experiences; my identity as a spiritual
being creates experiences of love and
fulfillment—true success.*

I know that if consciousness is focused exclusively on the outer world of form, the creative energy released will be totally conditioned by *human* consciousness, which includes the universal belief that "if anything can go wrong it will." However, I also know that if consciousness is predominantly spiritual, the energy expressed will be from the Mind of God within, which manifests as harmlessness, wholeness, abundance, fulfillment, and harmony. I have a choice—to live as a human being, or a spiritual being. My choice has been made.

DAY 7

*The creative energy radiating through my
conscious awareness of my Holy Self creates
experiences that correspond to that Self.*

My Divine Consciousness knows exactly what to do at every moment in time and space to fulfill every need, solve every problem, and lead me to the pinnacle of true success. It is doing this now through my awareness that It is doing so.

DAY 8

I am consciously aware of the activity of true success taking place in my Divine Consciousness. As within, so without.

The master plan for my success is in the Mind of my Holy Self right now, comprising ideal opportunities, open doors, helping hands—with everything coming together in perfect harmony.

DAY 9

I, the Holy Self within, have come that I might have life more abundant.

My Self is with me always, as the Reality of me, and through my awareness of the Presence, It has come that I may enjoy the fullness of the Kingdom. What is the abundant life to me? I let my faculty of spiritual imagination show me now. I see the perfect vision through the eyes of Spirit.

DAY 10

I declare my oneness with the Spirit of God I AM.

There has never been any separation from my True Nature, for there is only one Self. The thought of separation caused by ego has been dissolved, and I see my Self as I really am.

DAY 11

I declare my oneness with true success.

All that my Holy Self is, I am; all that my Holy Self has, is mine. I am *success*.

DAY 12

I declare my oneness with abundant supply.

I am one with every form and experience flowing from the Fountain of All-Good within.

DAY 13

I declare my oneness with creative wisdom.

I intuitively know that which is mine to do this day, and I do it with joy and enthusiasm.

DAY 14

I am radiating the success of my Divine Self.
A mighty river of grand success flows through
me into perfect manifestation.

I know that my Divine Self is like cascading waters, flowing in all directions, eternally expressing the All-Good.

DAY 15

I am radiating the abundance of my Divine Self.

I feel the dynamic radiation of energy, and see with my inner eye this energy as light filling my world. I consciously cooperate with my Self by practicing the technique of *radiation*—radiating the attributes of Self.

DAY 16

I am radiating the wholeness of my Divine Self.

I am a mighty sun, shining with intensity.

DAY 17

All that I radiate, I attract. I am a mighty magnet for my good.

I understand that the people, events, situations, conditions, and circumstances that correspond to my Self-awareness are brought to me through the

Law of Attractions. I am also aware that the Law goes into effect through the radiation process. What I radiate through my conscious awareness of the Master Self within comes back to me multiplied and overflowing.

DAY 18

I observe with unconditional love and discernment the activities of the phenomenal world, knowing I am not a part of that world.

I am assuming the role of the beholder. I witness the law of cause and effect in operation as I see individuals and groups sow and reap from many levels of consciousness. I observe all without judgment, not labeling anything good or bad.

DAY 19

There is a Divine Plan of true success for me, that which I came to do. I am ready and willing to accomplish my mission.

I know that I came into this world to serve in a special way, to create according to my own individual uniqueness. I now dedicate my life to this purpose.

DAY 20

I am a mind aware of its Self, holding steady in the radiating Light of my Self, ready to participate in the action of Self according to the understanding and guidance received.

This is spiritual understanding—to recognize that Self-awareness is a consciousness functioning as an open channel for the spiritual energy of Divine Mind, and knowing that this energy will transmute understanding from human to spiritual.

DAY 21

I practice harmlessness in every activity of my life.

When I practice harmlessness, I am free to live as the Master Self, for I have entered a state of mind where Goodwill is the motive behind all activity.

DAY 22

Those who have rejected me, who have hurt me, who have not recognized my true worth, I send my love to you with no conditions attached.

I love everyone for Who and What they are, without exceptions. I am the mighty power of God's love in radiant expression, and I let my love go before me to heal and harmonize every condition in my life.

DAY 23

My intention is to realize the Spirit of God within as my Source, Supply, Support, and Success.

This is my goal, and it has the full power of God's will behind it. I shall not fail.

DAY 24

The Spirit within performs the thing that is appointed for me. My Holy Self knows exactly what to do and is doing it now.

The responsibility for living my life has shifted from ego to Spirit. My role now is to keep my mind on the indwelling Presence and follow the guidance from within.

DAY 25

God's will is the only power in my life, and harmony reigns supreme.

I am now an Agent for God, a distributor of the Divine Energies, and a Co-creator with Spirit—continually alert to new instructions and assignments as a participant in the Creative Process.

DAY 26

*My consciousness of Spirit as my success
is my success.*

It is through the recognition of the already-present fullness of success within that a channel is opened for the manifestation of a totally success-ful life.

DAY 27

I am the energy of victory and triumph.

I have emerged victoriously as the conqueror of limited conditions and restricted situations. I now stand in quiet serenity, beholding the triumph of the Master Self I AM.

DAY 28

What I want for myself, I want for everyone.

I understand that a selfish intention is not honored. I am part of the Whole, and I see success omnipresent—a part of the Divine Plan for everyone.

DAY 29

I know now that nothing is impossible. The Spirit within has made all things new.

I have seen what the Great Reality within can do, and I now understand Omnipotence as never before.

DAY 30

This is just the beginning. I can now do ALL things through the Spirit of God I AM.

I now live and move and have my being in the Light of my Holy Self. I have moved from "I of myself can do nothing" to "I can do all things through Christ." And now I understand that I AM and HAVE all things, for there is but one Presence and one Power operating in my life. I AM *Success*. I AM *Fulfillment*.

(Tomorrow begin the second 30-day cycle)

At the end of the 60-day period, write down again what you consider complete success in your life and compare it with the original statement of your ideas of good fortune, triumph, and fulfillment. If you have been faithful in your daily work, you will not only see that success has come into your life as new forms and experiences, but also that your consciousness of what true success really means has changed. This is Spirit's way of saying, "Do not limit yourself, for you are an unlimited being."

Say to yourself:

I am enjoying the fullness of unlimited success, for I am in my true place, doing what I love and loving what I do, for the good of all.

And it is so!

NOTES

NOTES

NOTES

NOTES

NOTES

❧❧ ABOUT THE AUTHOR

John Randolph Price is an internationally known author and lecturer. Formerly a CEO in the corporate world, he has devoted over 25 years to researching the philosophic mysteries of ancient wisdom and incorporating those revelations in the writing of more than a dozen books. His work has earned national and international awards for humanitarianism, progress toward global peace, and contributing to a higher degree of positive living throughout the world.

In 1981, he and his wife, Jan, formed The Quartus Foundation, a spiritual research and communications organization.

For information about workshops conducted by John and Jan Price, and their monthly publications, please contact:

The Quartus Foundation
P.O. Box 1768, Boerne, TX 78006
(830) 249-3985
(830) 249-3318 (fax)